CentOS 7.3 Linux Server Guide

Table of Contents

Introduction

Most companies and organizations are more concerned about the security of the data. This also applies to individuals who use computers. Linux servers offer you the best kind of security for your data. Despite the issue of security, Linux servers also offer you a high rate of performance. This means that there is much that you can do with your Linux server compared to what you can do with the desktop versions of Linux. This is why you should familiarize yourself with how to use the Linux servers. This book is an excellent guide for you on how to use the CentOS 73 Linux server. It guides you from the basic steps to the most advanced steps of setting up and using the various software in this system. Enjoy reading!

Chapter 1- Installation

We will show how you can install the CentOS 7.3 on a machine which is based on UEFI. Begin by entering the motherboard UEFI settings simply by pressing the special key (either F1, F11, or F12 based on the specifications of your motherboard). Also, ensure that you have disabled the options for QuickBoot/FastBoot and Secure Boot.

The installation can then be done by following the steps given below:

1. Begin by downloading the CentOS 7.3 ISO image. You can find this by clicking here. Once the download is complete, burn the image to a DVD or just makes a bootable USB Drive which is compatible with UEFI. This can be done by use of the Rufus utility.

   Just put the USB/DVD in an appropriate motherboard drive, and then reboot the machine and instruct BIOS/UEFI to boot-up from DVD/USB simply by pressing the special function key (either F12 or F10 based on specifications of the vendor).

   After the ISO image has booted, you will see the first screen on the machine output. You can choose "Install CentOS 7" from the menu and then hit "Enter" so as to continue.

2. Now that the image has been loaded into the RAM of the machine, you will see the welcome screen. Choose the language which you need to use, and then click on the "Continue" button.

WELCOME TO CENTOS 7.

What language would you like to use during the installation process?

English	English >	English (United States)
Afrikaans	Afrikaans	English (United Kingdom
አማርኛ	Amharic	English (India)
العربية	Arabic	English (Australia)
অসমীয়া	Assamese	English (Canada)
Asturianu	Asturian	English (Denmark)
Беларуская	Belarusian	English (Ireland)
Български	Bulgarian	English (New Zealand)
বাংলা	Bengali	English (Nigeria)
Bosanski	Bosnian	English (Hong Kong SAF
Català	Catalan	English (Philippines)
Čeština	Czech	English (Singapore)
Cymraeg	Welsh	English (South Africa)
Dansk	Danish	English (Zambia)
		English (Zimbabwe)
		English (Botswana)

3. Choose the Date and Time, and then select the geographical location from the provided map. Once the date and time are set to the correct ones, click on the "Done" button so that you can be taken back to the installations screen.

4. Hit on the keyboard menu so as to setup the layout for the keyboard. Add or choose a keyboard layout, and then click on "Done" so as to continue.

5. Configure or add the system language support, and then click on "Done" so as to continue.

Select additional language support to be installed:

English	English ›	☑ English (United States)
Español	Spanish	☐ English (United Kingdom)
Eesti	Estonian	☐ English (India)
Euskara	Basque	☐ English (Australia)
فارسی	Persian	☐ English (Canada)
		☐ English (Denmark)
Suomi	Finnish	☐ English (Ireland)
Français	French	☐ English (New Zealand)
Galego	Galician	☐ English (Nigeria)
ગુજરાતી	Gujarati	☐ English (Hong Kong SAR China)
हिन्दी	Hindi	☐ English (Philippines)
Hrvatski	Croatian	☐ English (Singapore)
Magyar	Hungarian	☐ English (South Africa)
Interlingua	Interlingua	☐ English (Zambia)
Bahasa Indonesia	Indonesian	☐ English (Zimbabwe)
Íslenska	Icelandic	☐ English (Botswana)
Italiano	Italian	☐ English (Antigua & Barbuda)

6. In the next step, you will be allowed to setup the "Security Policy" for your system by selecting a security profile from the provided list.

   You just have to click on the "Select profile" button so as to choose the security profile which you desire. You can then turn ON your Apply Security policy button. You can then click on the "Done" button so as to proceed with the installation.

7. In the next step, it will be time for you to configure the environment for the base machine by clicking on the "Software Selection" button. Since we need a server, ensure that you choose the kind of server which you will need to be using and it will be installed.

   For you to be able to do a subsequent customization of your system, just choose "Minimal Install," and then click on the "Done" button so as to proceed.

8. If you need to get a server with a Graphical User Interface, select "Server with GUI" which can be found on the left pane and then check for the right add-ons from the right panel, and this will be determined by the services which your server will be offering to the network clients.

9. If you are not using any other specific network locations, you should leave Installation Source as the default. You can then click on the "Installation Destination" so as to create the hard disk partitions.
On the screen for Device selection, ensure that you have checked the local machine hard disk.

10. You can click on the KDUMP option, and then disable it if you are in need of some free RAM in the system. Finish this by clicking on the "Done" button, and you will be taken back to the installation screen.

11. Set the hostname for your machine, and then enable the network service. Click on "Network & Hostname," and type the Fully Qualified Domain Name for your system on the Host Name, and then activate the network interface by turning the Ethernet button to ON if there is a DHCP server in the LAN.

12. Click on the "Configure" button so as to statically configure the network, add the IP settings manually. Apply the changes made by clicking on the "Save" button. You can then click on the "Done" button, and you will be taken back to the installer page.

13. You can then review all the configurations which you have made, and once you are sure everything is okay, click on the "Begin Installation" button so that the installation process can begin.

14. Once the process of installation has started, you will get to see a new screen for setting up the users. Click on

ROOT PASSWORD, and create a very strong password for the root account. Once done, click on the "Done" button so that you can get back to the installation screen.

15. Note that it is not advisable for you to use your system from the root account. You should create some new user by clicking on the "User Creation" button. Enter the details for this new user, while ensuring that all the options are enabled so that you may be prompted to enter a password whenever you need to log into the system. Once done, click on the "Done" button and the installation process will be completed.

16. You will then see the installer reporting that the CentOS have been successfully installed. For you to be able to use this system, just remove the installation media and then reboot your machine.

17. Once the system reboots, use your credentials so as to log into the system, and then execute the following command so as to update your system fully:

$ sudo yum update

For all the questions you will be asked by the package manager, just answer with yes. Once the update has been done, just reboot your system so that the changes can be applied to the kernel.

Chapter 2- Installing Memcached

Memcached is an object caching system for distributed memory which is generic in nature and offers a high performance. It was originally developed so as to help in speeding up the dynamic web applications simply by alleviating the database load. This tool also has other uses. This tool helps to do a quick deployment, as well as an easy development, and you can use it to solve a number of problems which are associated with large data caches. To install its package in your CentOS 7.3 server, run the following command:

yum install memcached

The command will install the package in your machine. The next step should be for you to configure this. The most important part for you to configure is the CACHESIZE. This represents the size of the cache in megabytes. This calls for you to edit the /etc/sysconfig/memcached file. Consider the configuration given below, which makes it use a size of 512 MB:

PORT="11211"
USER="memcached"
MAXCONN="1024"
CACHESIZE="512"
OPTIONS=""

Start the Memcached on your CentOS by running the following commands:

systemctl start memcached.service ## restart is used after the update

 systemctl enable memcached.service

Remember that our Memcached was running on the port number 11211. We can use that port so as to check whether the Memcached is running or not. This is shown below:

```
echo stats | nc localhost 11211
STAT pid 7599
STAT uptime 10
STAT time 1265288542
STAT version 1.4.4
STAT pointer_size 32
STAT rusage_user 0.003999
STAT rusage_system 0.052991
STAT curr_connections 10
STAT total_connections 11
STAT connection_structures 11
STAT cmd_get 0
STAT cmd_set 0
STAT cmd_flush 0
STAT get_hits 0
STAT get_misses 0
STAT delete_misses 0
STAT delete_hits 0
STAT incr_misses 0
STAT incr_hits 0
STAT decr_misses 0
STAT decr_hits 0
STAT cas_misses 0
STAT cas_hits 0
STAT cas_badval 0
STAT auth_cmds 0
STAT auth_errors 0
STAT bytes_read 6
STAT bytes_written 0
STAT limit_maxbytes 536870912
STAT accepting_conns 1
STAT listen_disabled_num 0
STAT threads 4
STAT conn_yields 0
STAT bytes 0
STAT curr_items 0
STAT total_items 0
STAT evictions 0
```

END

Let us to get some value from this. We have to use the following command:

echo get some_value | nc localhost 11211
END

No value was found. We can check for the statistics once again:

echo stats | nc localhost 11211
STAT pid 7599
STAT uptime 10
STAT time 1265288542
STAT version 1.4.4
[...]
STAT cmd_get 1
STAT cmd_set 0
STAT cmd_flush 0
STAT get_hits 0
STAT get_misses 1
STAT delete_misses 0
[...]
STAT evictions 0
END

The output clearly shows that the Memcached is running okay. We can then go ahead to use some web application for testing the Mecached. Begin by opening the Memcached port, that is, 11211, on the Iptables firewall. First, list all the firewall zones which are active. The following command will help achieve this:

firewall-cmd --get-active-zones

You should get an output which is closely related to the one shown below:

public

interfaces: wlp1s0

A new rule should then be added to the firewalld. The following command can help you to do this:

firewall-cmd --permanent --zone=public --add --port=11211/tcp

Now that you have made some changes, you should enable them by restarting the firewalld.service. The following command can help you to achieve this:

systemctl restart firewalld.service

You can then use the command given below so as to test for the remote connection:

echo stats | nc memcache_host_name_or_ip 11211

The next step should involve the installation of the Memcached PHP Module or the Memcache to your CentOS server. The following command can help you install the Memcache module and the PHP:

yum install php php-pecl-memcache

The Memcached module and the PHP can then be installed as follows:

yum install php php-pecl-memcached

Restart the web server by running the following command:

/etc/init.d/httpd restart
OR
service httpd restart

Chapter 3- Installing Nginx

Nginx is web server software which offers a very high performance. When compared to the Apache HTTP server, it is a bit flexible and more lightweight.

In this chapter, we will show you how to install this server software on a CentOS 73 server. For you to be able to install this, you must have root privileges for the account you are using.

The first step should involve addition of the Nginx repository. For you to CentOS 7 EPEL repository, just launch the terminal and then run the following command:

sudo yum install epel-release

The command will help you to install the Nginx repository into your server. You can then run the following command so as to install the Nginx:

sudo yum install nginx

When prompted for an answer, just type "yes," and the installation of the Nginx will be done on your virtual private server.

Note that once the Nginx has been installed, it will not start on its own. You have to start it by typing the following command:

sudo systemctl start nginx

You may be using a firewall in your system. If this is the case, there is a need for you to allow traffic from both HTTP and HTTPS protocols. This can be achieved by executing the command given below:

sudo firewall-cmd --permanent --zone=public --add-service=http

sudo firewall-cmd --permanent --zone=public --add-service=https

sudo firewall-cmd –reload

A spot check will be good for you to be sure that everything is running as you expected. You just have to visit the public IP address of your server in the web browser. If you are not aware of the IP address, look for the way to know it.

http://server_domain_name_or_IP/

The default web page for the CentOS 7 Nginx will be opened. This is usually provided to give you all the necessary information and help you do the testing. If you see the welcome page, just know that the server is okay and running well.

It will also be good for you to enable the Nginx so that it can start automatically once the system is booted. You just have to run the following command:

sudo systemctl enable nginx

You will have installed the Nginx and it is now running.

Finding the IP Address of Your Server

To know the IP address of your server, begin by looking for the network interfaces of your machine simply by executing the following command:

ip addr

In my case, I get the following:

1. lo: <LOOPBACK,UP,LOWER_UP> mtu 65536 qdisc noqueue state UNKNOWN

. . .
**2: eth0:
<BROADCAST,MULTICAST,UP,LOWER_UP> mtu
1500 qdisc pfifo_fast state UP qlen 1000**

. . .

The number of interfaces shown in this case will be determined by the hardware number that you have on your machine. The interface named "lo" represents the loopback interface, but we are not interested in this interface. However, the interface "eth0" represents the Ethernet interface, and this is what we are interested in.

Now that you are aware of the interface name, there is a command which you can run so that you may know the IP address of your server. This is shown below:

ip addr show eth0 | grep inet | awk '{ print $2; }' | sed 's/\/.*$//'

For you to start serving own application or pages through the Nginx, you have to know where the default server root directory and the Nginx configuration files are located.

Your default server root directory should be in the /usr/share/nginx/html location. Any files which are placed in the directory have to be served on the web server. Such a location has to be specified in in default server block configuration file which comes with the Nginx, and this can be found in the "/etc/nginx/conf.d/default.conf" directory.

Other additional server blocks, which are referred to as the Virtual Hosts in Apache, may be added by having to create some new configuration files in the /etc/nginx/conf.d. Any file which .conf in this directory will have to be loaded at the time the Nginx is being started.

The main configuration file for the Nginx can be found in /etc/nginx/nginx.conf. Settings should be changed from here, such as the user who is allowed to execute the Nginx daemon processes, and the worker processes number which will get spawned when the Nginx is running.

Chapter 4- Setting up MongoDB

MongoDb is a NoSQL database, but it is document oriented. It is used for storing documents which are the same as JSON in terms of their structure. It offers a high performance and it scales well. In this chapter, we will show you how to install this in your CentOS 7.3 server:

Adding the Repository

The default state is that there is no MongoDB repository in the CentOS. This is why this should be added to the local machine. Begin by opening the file "/etc/yum.repos.d/mongodb-org.repo" in a text editor such as VIM. Just execute the following command:

 # vi /etc/yum.repos.d/mongodb-org.repo

This will give you the following output:

[mongodb-org-3.2]
name=MongoDB Repository
baseurl=https://repo.mongodb.org/yum/redhat/$rel
easever/mongodb-org/3.2/x86_64/

gpgcheck=1
enabled=1gpgkey=https://www.mongodb.org/static/
pgp/server-3.2.asc

Make sure that your file looks as shown above. Once the repository has been added to the local machine, we have to update the system so that our yum command can pull and check for the repository information. Just run the "yum update" command as shown below:

 # yum update
Output:
Loaded plugins: fastestmirror
base   **| 3.6 kB   00:00**

```
extras                          | 3.4 kB   00:00
mongodb-org-3.2                        | 2.5 kB
00:00
updates                         | 3.4 kB   00:00
mongodb-org-3.2/7/primary_db              | 54
kB  00:01
Determining fastest mirrors
 * base: mirror.dhakacom.com
 * extras: mirror.dhakacom.com
 * updates: mirror.dhakacom.com
No packages marked for update
```

You will then have updated the system. Now that the repository is setup, we can go ahead and begin to install the MongoDB.

Install MongoDB

At this point, it is possible for us to install the MongoDB on our machine. The installation can be done by use of the yum command. Just run the command given below:

 # yum install mongodb-org

Below is a section of the last few lines from the command's output:

Retrieving key from
https://www.mongodb.org/static/pgp/server-3.2.asc

Importing GPG key 0xEA312927:
 Userid   : "MongoDB 3.2 Release Signing Key <packaging@mongodb.com>"

 Fingerprint: 42f3 e95a 2c4f 0827 9c49 60ad d68f a50f ea31 2927
 From   :
https://www.mongodb.org/static/pgp/server-3.2.asc
Is this ok [y/N]:y

Running transaction check
Running transaction test
Transaction test succeeded
Running transaction
  Installing : mongodb-org-server-3.2.11-
1.el7.x86_64   1/5

  Installing : mongodb-org-mongos-3.2.11-
1.el7.x86_64   2/5

  Installing : mongodb-org-tools-3.2.11-
1.el7.x86_64   3/5

  Installing : mongodb-org-shell-3.2.11-
1.el7.x86_64   4/5

  Installing : mongodb-org-3.2.11-1.el7.x86_64
              5/5
  Verifying : mongodb-org-shell-3.2.11-
1.el7.x86_64   1/5

  Verifying : mongodb-org-tools-3.2.11-
1.el7.x86_64   2/5

  Verifying : mongodb-org-mongos-3.2.11-
1.el7.x86_64   3/5

  Verifying : mongodb-org-server-3.2.11-
1.el7.x86_64   4/5

  Verifying : mongodb-org-3.2.11-
1.el7.x86_64   5/5
Installed:

  mongodb-org.x86_64 0:3.2.11-1.el7
Dependency Installed:
  mongodb-org-mongos.x86_64 0:3.2.11-1.el7
  mongodb-org-server.x86_64 0:3.2.11-1.el7
  mongodb-org-shell.x86_64 0:3.2.11-1.el7

mongodb-org-tools.x86_64 0:3.2.11-1.el7

Complete!

Once you see the "Complete!", just know that everything is now okay. Note that during the installation process, you will be prompted, and for you to continue, you only have to type "yes." Now that MongoDB has been installed, we can go ahead and install the MongoDB services. The following command can help us start these services:

 # systemctl start mongod

Also though we have started the services, it is good for us to check for their status so as to be sure about it. Just run the command given below:

 # systemctl status mongod

The output from the command should be related to what is given below:

mongod.service - SYSV: Mongo is a scalable, document-oriented database.

Loaded: loaded (/etc/rc.d/init.d/mongod)
Active: active (running) since Wed 2017 11-02-22 11:09:12 IST; 12s ago

Docs: man:systemd-sysv-generator(8)
Process: 9901 ExecStart=/etc/rc.d/init.d/mongod start (code=exited, status=0/SUCCESS)

CGroup: /system.slice/mongod.service
└─9912 /usr/bin/mongod -f /etc/mongod.conf
Feb 22 11:09:22 localhost.localdomain systemd[1]: Starting SYSV: Mongo is a s...

Feb 22 11:09:22 localhost.localdomain runuser[9908]: pam_unix(runuser:session...

Feb 22 11:09:22 localhost.localdomain runuser[9908]: pam_unix(runuser:session...

Feb 22 11:09:22 localhost.localdomain mongod[9901]: Starting mongod: [OK]

Feb 22 11:09:22 localhost.localdomain systemd[1]: Started SYSV: Mongo is a sc...Hint: Some lines were ellipsized, use -l to show in full.

MongoDB will now have been installed into the system. We can then reload the configuration by executing the command given below:

 # systemctl reload mongod

Use the following command so as to stop the MongoDB service:

 # systemctl stop mongod

Configuring the Number of Processes

The number of processes is usually set to as low as 4096. Try to run the "mongo" command as shown below:

 # mongo

The command will give you an error as shown below:

MongoDB shell version: 3.2.11
connecting to: test
Welcome to the MongoDB shell.
For interactive help, type "help".
For more comprehensive documentation, see
http://docs.mongodb.org/

Questions? Try the support group
http://groups.google.com/group/mongodb-user
Server has startup warnings:
2017-02-22T11:09:21.553+0530 I CONTROL [initandlisten] ** WARNING: soft rlimits too low. rlimits set to 4096 processes, 64000 files. Number of processes should be at least 32000 : 0.5 times number of files.

2017-02-22T14:09:25.553+0530 I CONTROL [initandlisten]

For us to do a configuration on the number of processes which are needed, we have to edit the file named "20-nproc.conf." This file can be found at "/etc/security/limits.d/." Execute the following command so as to open it in the vim editor:

vi /etc/security/limits.d/20-nproc.conf

You will see the following output from the above command:

Default limit for number of user's processes to prevent

accidental fork bombs.
See rhbz #432903 for reasoning.
*   soft   nproc   4096
root   soft   nproc   unlimited

We should change the value of 4096 to 32000. This is shown below:

*   soft   nproc   32000

Now that the above value has been changed, we have to restart our MongoDB service so that the changes can take effect. The following command will help you to restart the system:

systemctl restart mongod

The command will restart the system, and you will be prompted for the password so as to login again!

Creation of Administrator User

We need to create the administrator user for our MongoDB password. The name for the user will be "admin," and the corresponding password will be "userpass." Once the user has been created, we will check whether they are available in the database or not. The following steps will help us create the user: Type the "mongo" command on the terminal:

 # mongo

This will give the following output:

MongoDB shell version: 3.2.11
connecting to: test

Type the command "use admin" as shown below:

> use admin
switched to db admin

You can type the following code in the terminal:

db.createUser(
... {
...   user: "admin",
...   pwd: "userpass",
...   roles: [{ role: "userAdminAnyDatabase", db: "admin" }]

... }
...)
Successfully added user: {
"user" : "admin",
"roles" : [

```
{
"role" : "userAdminAnyDatabase",
"db" : "admin"
}
]
}
```

We are informed that the user has been created, and then added to the system. The role assigned to this means that he will be in a position to perform an administration task on any database contained in the MongoDB. We can then run the following command so as to know the users who are available in the database, and this will let us know whether or not the user was created:

```
> show users;
{
"_id" : "admin.admin",
"user" : "admin",
"db" : "admin",
"roles" : [
{
"role" : "userAdminAnyDatabase",
"db" : "admin"
}
]
}
>
```

That is it! You will be done. You have learned how to install the MongoDb database to your CentOS 7.3 server, how to change the process number from 4096 to 32000 as well as how to add some new user. We created an admin user for the system!

Chapter 5- Lemp Setup

LEMP (Linux, Nginx, MySQL, PHP) is a group of software (open source) which are installed together so as to enable the server host web apps and dynamic websites.

The term is simply an acronym representing the Linux operating system, the ENginix web server which acts as a replacement for the Apache web server used in LAMP.

The data for the site has to be stored in a MySQL database which makes use of MariaDB and the PHP is used for processing the dynamic content. In this chapter, we will be showing you how to setup this in your CentOS 7.3 server.

Before we can begin the installation process, you should ensure that you have some non-root account which has already been setup in your server. You can then follow the steps given below so as to perform the installation:

Installing Nginx

For us to be able to display the web pages to the visitors of our site, we have to use Nginx, which is a modern and efficient web server. Remember that we discussed the installation of Nginx in our previous chapter. If you had not done those steps, just follow them again so as to install Nginx. Once the installation is complete and the services started, just find the IP address of your server. You will then be done with this step.

Installing MySQL (MariaDB)

Since our web server is now running, we can go ahead to install MariaDB, which is a replacement for MySQL. MAriaDb is just a community-developed fork for the MySQL relational database management system. It provides us with a way of accessing where our system can store and access information.

This software can be obtained and installed by the use of the yum command. We will also take advantage and install some helper software which will help us facilitate communication between the components. Just run the following command on the terminal:

sudo yum install mariadb-server mariadb

The command will install MariaDB in our system. Once the installation is complete, it will be good for us to restart MariaDB. This can simply be done by executing the following command:

sudo yum install mariadb-server mariadb

At this point, we will have our database up and running as we expected.

We can then go ahead and then execute a security script which will remove some of the defaults which endanger the system, and it will disable the access to the database system somehow. Just run the following command so as to launch the interactive script:

sudo mysql_secure_installation

You will be prompted to enter the root password. Since we have just installed MySQL into our system, it is more likely that you will not have the root password, so just leave it blank by pressing the enter key. You will then be asked whether you need to set up the root password. Just type Y, and then follow the instructions given below:

mysql_secure_installation prompts:
Enter current password for root (enter for none):
OK, successfully used password, moving on...

Setting the root password ensures that nobody can log into the MariaDB. Root user without the proper authorisation.

New password: userpass
Re-enter new password: userpass
Password updated successfully!
Reloading privilege tables..
... Success!

In the case of the other settings, you should accept the default values by hitting the enter key. With this, some sample users and databases will be removed, the remote logins will be disabled, and the new rules will be loaded so that the newly made changes will be respected by MySQL.

With that, we should enable MariaDB to be started once the system is booted. The following command will help us achieve it:

sudo systemctl enable mariadb

You will have setup your database system and be ready to move on.

Installing PHP

The PHP will be responsible for processing and displaying our dynamic content. It is able to process our scripts, establish a connection to the MySQL database so as to obtain information, and this information is passed to the web server so that it can be displayed.

Our yum system can be leveraged so that the components can be installed. The packages php-mysql and php-fpm will also be included. Just run the following command:

sudo yum install php php-mysql php-fpm

Configuring the PHP Processor

Now that the PHP processor has been installed into our system, it will be good for us to go ahead and configure it so that everything can remain secure. You should open the php-fpm configuration file in your vi editor by use of root privileges. You just have to run the following command:

sudo vi /etc/php.ini

The file will then be opened in the vim editor. We are looking for the parameter which can be used for setting cgi.fix_pathinfo. You will find it has been commented out by use of a semicolon (;), and its default value has been set to 1. This setting is for telling the PHP to run or execute any script which is closest if the PHP file fails to match exactly.

This setting is very dangerous. With such a setting, it is possible for malicious users to design PHP scripts and execute them even if they are not allowed to be executed, hence putting our system at risk.To change this setting, we have to uncomment the line by removing the semicolon and then set its value to 0. This is shown below:

cgi.fix_pathinfo=0

Once you have changed the line to the above, just save and then close the file. You can then go ahead and then open ww.conf, which is the php-fpm configuration file. The following command will help you to open up this file in the vi editor:

sudo vi /etc/php-fpm.d/www.conf

You can then look for a line specifying the "listen" parameter and then change it so that it can be as shown below:

listen = /var/run/php-fpm/php-fpm.sock

Next, just look for the lines which specify the parameters listen.owner and listen.group and then uncomment them. After this, they should look as shown below:

listen.owner = nobody
listen.group = nobody

You can then look for parameters which have been used for specifying the user and the group and then change their value from "apache" to "nginx." This is shown below:

user = nginx
group = nginx

You can then save the file and quit. Go ahead and run the following command so as to restart the PHP processor:

sudo systemctl start php-fpm

The changes which are needed will have been made. You can then go ahead and enable the php-fpm so that it can be started after booting up the system. You just have to run the command given below:

sudo systemctl enable php-fpm

Nginx Configuration

At this point, we have all the necessary components installed. We should go ahead to configure Nginx so that it can make use of the PHP processor for processing of the dynamic content.

This has to be done on the server block level. Just type the following command so as to open the default configuration file for the Nginx server block:

sudo vi /etc/nginx/conf.d/default.conf

When the comments are removed, you should find the following content in the file:

```
server {
    listen      80;
    server_name  localhost;

    location / {
        root  /usr/share/nginx/html;
        index  index.html index.htm;
    }
    error_page  500 502 503 504  /50x.html;
    location = /50x.html {
        root  /usr/share/nginx/html;
    }
}
```

There are a number of changes which need to be made to our site via this file. The option index.php has to be added so that it can be the first value for the index directive so that the PHP index files can be served once a directory has been requested.

The directive "server_name" should also be modified so that it can point to the IP address of our server or its domain name.

Our real configuration file has some lines which have been commented out, and these are used for processing the error routines. We should uncomment lines so that we can take advantage of the functionality. For the actual PHP processing to take place, there is also another section which has to be uncommented. The "try_files" directive should also be added so that Nginx may not pass the bad requests to the PHP processor.

The updated "/etc/nginx/conf.d/default.conf" configuration file should then appear as shown below:

```
server {
    listen      80;
```

```
server_name server_domain_name_or_IP;

# note that these lines are originally from the
"location /" block

root   /usr/share/nginx/html;
index index.php index.html index.htm;

location / {
   try_files $uri $uri/ =404;
}
error  page 404 /404.html;
error_page 500 502 503 504 /50x.html;
location = /50x.html {
   root /usr/share/nginx/html;
}

location ~ \.php$ {
   try_files $uri =404;
   fastcgi_pass unix:/var/run/php-fpm/php-
fpm.sock;

   fastcgi_index index.php;
   fastcgi_param SCRIPT_FILENAME
$document_root$fastcgi_script_name;

   include fastcgi_params;
   }
}
```

Now that you have the changes as shown above, you can save the file and then close it. You can use the following command to restart the Nginx and then apply the changes you have just made:

sudo systemctl restart nginx

Testing

It is now time for us to test whether or not our system has been configured correctly. This calls for us to create a basic script and then use it for testing purposes. This script will be given the name "info.php." For the Apache server to locate this file and then use it correctly, it must be kept in a certain directory, which is the "web root" directory. This directory can be found at "/usr/share/nginx/html/." To create the file in the directory, you just have to run the following command:

sudo vi /usr/share/nginx/html/info.php

The above command will open the file in the vim text editor. You can then add the following PHP line of code to it:

<?php phpinfo(); ?>

Once done, just save it, and then quit the file. It is now time for us to test whether our server is capable of displaying the content which is coming from a PHP script. This can be done simply by opening the page on a web browser. The public IP address of the server will be needed for us to do this. Just open your browser, and then type the following url in the url section:

http://your_server_IP_address/info.php

Note that you have to replace the above with the public IP address of your server. You will then see the PHP welcome page which begins as follows:

Other than the PHP version which you are using, you will also see other details regarding the same. It is simply the information about the server when viewed from the PHP. It

34

will help you for debugging purposes and it will help you to be sure that all settings are they are supposed to be. If you see the above page in your system, you can be sure that everything is okay, meaning that you have succeeded in setting this up.

However, the file puts the system at a security risk. This is because unauthorized users may access it and gain information regarding our server. This calls for us to remove this file. The following command can help us achieve this:

sudo rm /usr/share/nginx/html/info.php

However, in case you need to get the same information later, you can feel free to recreate the file and you will access the information. You will have successfully installed the LEMP stack on your system, and now there are number of options for you to select. This software can allow you to install a number of web software programs and websites on your system.

Chapter 6- Setting up RabbitMQ

RabbitMQ is message broker software which I used for implementation of the Advanced Message Queuing Protocol (AMQP). It is available as an open source software program. This software is capable of running on a majority of the modern operating systems. It is possible for you to install this software in your CentOS 7.3 server. This can be done as outlined in the following step:

Note that the RabbitMQ was developed by use of the Erlang programming language. This is why one should first install Erlang before they can install the RabbitMQ.

Install Erlang

Note that Erlang is just a programming language which is highly used for building real time systems which are massively required. Before beginning to install it, first execute the following commands:

yum update
yum install epel-release
yum install gcc gcc-c++ glibc-devel make ncurses-devel openssl-devel autoconf java-1.8.0-openjdk-devel git wget wxBase.x86_64

We don't need to get Erlang from our official repositories, as these might have an old version of this. Our aim is to get the latest version, so we should download and then install it. Just open the official repository page for Elarng and then download the latest available version.

Remember that our intention is to install the Erlang repository in a CentOS server. This is why the following repository has to be added:

wget http://packages.erlang-solutions.com/erlang-solutions-1.0-1.noarch.rpm

rpm -Uvh erlang-solutions-1.0-1.noarch.rpm

You can then run the following command so as to update the lists in the repository:

yum update

Run the following command so as to install Erlang:

yum install erlang

The above command should install Erlang into your system. However, it is good for you to verify and be sure that the installation was successful. To do this, run the following command:

Erl

A sample output from the command should appear as shown below:

Erlang/OTP 18 [erts-7.3] [source-d2a6d81] [64-bit] [async-threads:10] [hipe] [kernel-poll:false]

Eshell V7.3 (abort with ^G)
1>

If you see the Erlang command prompt, just know that the installation was successful. If you need to close this shell, just click on Ctrl + C (^C). We can then test whether Erlang is running as it should. Just create a file named "hello.erl." Open the terminal, and run the following command

vi hello.erl

Add the following lines of code to your file:

-module(hello).

```
-export([hello_world/0]).
hello_world() -> io:fwrite("hello, world!\n").
```

Save your file, and then close it. Enter the Erlang shell by typing the following command:

Erl

You can then execute the following two commands:

```
c(hello).
hello:hello_world().
```

Remember to add the dots at the end of the commands as shown above. Otherwise, you will get an error. You will get the "hello, world!" salutation printed on the terminal.

Installing RabbitMQ

Now that Erlang has been installed, we can go ahead to install RabbitMQ. Use the following command so as to download it:

$ wget https://www.rabbitmq.com/releases/rabbitmq-**server/v3.6.1/rabbitmq-server-3.6.1-1.noarch.rpm**

You can then run the command given below so as to add the signing key for RabbitMQ:

rpm --import https://www.rabbitmq.com/rabbitmq-signing-key-public.asc

You can then run the following command so as to install the RabitMQ server:

yum install rabbitmq-server-3.6.1-1.noarch.rpm

The command will give you output similar to the one given below:

```
Loaded plugins: fastestmirror
Examining rabbitmq-server-3.6.1-1.noarch.rpm:
rabbitmq-server-3.6.1-1.noarch

Marking rabbitmq-server-3.6.1-1.noarch.rpm to be
installed

Resolving Dependencies
--> Running transaction check
---> Package rabbitmq-server.noarch 0:3.6.1-1 will be
installed

--> Finished Dependency Resolution

Dependencies Resolved

=========================================
=========================================
==
 Package Arch Version Repository Size
=========================================
=========================================
==
Installing:
 rabbitmq-server noarch 3.6.1-1 /rabbitmq-server-
3.6.1-1.noarch 5.5 M

Transaction Summary
=========================================
=========================================
==
Install 1 Package

Total size: 5.5 M
Installed size: 5.5 M
Is this ok [y/d/N]: y
```

As shown, once prompted, just type "y" for yes, and the installation will continue.

Accessing the Management Console

This tool is good for allowing you to monitor the server processes through a web browser. The RabbitMQ management console can be enabled by executing the following command:

rabbitmq-plugins enable rabbitmq_management

This should then be followed by the following command:

chown -R rabbitmq:rabbitmq /var/lib/rabbitmq/

You can then launch your browser and navigate to the URL given below so as to access the RabbitMQ server management console:

http://ip-address:15672/

Note that the RabbitMQ management console comes with a default username and password, which are "guest" and "guest." You may also go ahead and create the admin user if you need to have one. You only have to run the following commands:

rabbitmqctl add_user admin admin
rabbitmqctl set_user_tags admin administrator
rabbitmqctl set_permissions -p / admin ".*" ".*" ".*"

You can then enter the username as well as the password so as to gain access to the RabbitMQ web console. You will be taken to the web dashboard for RabbitMQ. You can then begin to use your RabbitMQ server!

Chapter 7- Node.js Setup

Node.js is simply a platform for JavaScript which can be used for programming on the server side. With this, users are able to create networked applications which are needed for backend functionality. When JavaScript is used as the language, both on the client and on the server side, the development process becomes much easy and consistent. Let us discuss how we can get Node.js running on our CentOS 7.3 server.

Installing Node from Source

A simple way of getting Node.js is getting its source code and then compiling it. The source has to be obtained from the website of the project. Once you are on the download page, just right click on the link for the source code and then choose "Copy link address" or any other related option you might be given. You can then use the "wget" command and the link on your server so as to download this as shown below:

wget http://nodejs.org/dist/v0.10.30/node-v0.10.30.tar.gz

You can then extract the archive you have just downloaded and then move to your new directory. This is shown below:

tar xzvf node-v* && cd node-v*

There will be a number of packages which should be downloaded from CentOS repositories so as to compile the code. You can obtain them by use of the "yum" command:

sudo yum install gcc gcc-c++

You can then configure and compile your software as follows:

./configure
Make

The process of compiling this will take some minutes, so be patient. Once the compilation is complete, you can install the software by running the following command:

sudo make install

If you need to verify whether the installation of Node.js was successful or not, just run the following command so as to check for its version:

node –version

The command will print the version of Node.js which has been installed into your system. If you see the version number, then you should know that the installation was successful in your case.

Installing Node.js from Node Site

It is possible for us to obtain the pre-built packages for Node from its official website and then install them. You should first obtain the link which has these binaries. After that, you should use this link together with the "wget" command so as to install the binaries. This is shown below:

cd ~
wget http://nodejs.org/dist/v0.10.30/node-v0.10.30-linux-x64.tar.gz

Note that I first used the change directory command so as to change directory to the home directory. Remember that the version number in your URL must not be the same as the one given above as this is the latest version just for now. Just use it as you obtained it from the link.

After the download is complete, we can extract the package into the local package hierarchy of the system by use of the "tar" command. Note that the archive is usually packaged in a versioned directory, and we can get rid of this by passing the option "--strip-components 1." We will use the "-c" option so as to specify the target directory in the command. This is shown below:

sudo tar --strip-components 1 -xzvf node-v* -C /usr/local

Note that after running the above command, all the components will be installed in the "/usr/local" directory or branch of the system. To verify whether the installation was successful or not, we only have to check for the version of Node in our system by running the following command:

node –version

If you see the version, just know that the installation was successful, and you can begin to use Node.js on your CentOS server.

Installation of Node from EPEL Repository

The Extra Packages for Enterprise Linux (EPEL) can help us with installation of Node.js, and this is available for CentOS and other Linux distributions. For you to be granted access to the EPEL repository, the repo-list for your installation has to be modified. The access to this repository can also be modified by installing a package known as "epel-release," and this is available in the current repos. The following command can help us install this package:

sudo yum install epel-release

This will grant you access to the EPEL repository. You can then go ahead and install Node.js by use of the yum command as shown below:

sudo yum install nodejs

The above command should install Node.js to your server, but it is good for you to confirm whether the installation was successful or not by running the command to query for the version:

node –version

Most people need to access the npm for the purpose of management of their packages. You can use the following command so as to get this from the EPEL:

sudo yum install npm

Installing Node Using Node Version Manager

The node version manager (nvm) also provides us with a more flexible way for installing Node.js. With this tool, you can install and then maintain a number of Node repositories, as well as other packages which are associated with it.

For you to install Node.js on your CentOS machine, you have to visit the project page on GitHub, and then copy the wget or curl command from the README file which will be displayed on main page. You will have obtained a pointer to the most recent point of the script.

Before you can pipe the command to bash, you should first audit your script to ensure that it will only do what you have agreed should be done. To do this, just do away with the "| bash" segment which is found at the end of the curl command. This is shown below:

curl
https://raw.githubusercontent.com/creationix/nvm/v0.13.1/install.sh

You should look at it closely and ensure that you are much comfortable with the changes which you have just made. If you become satisfied, just go ahead and then append the "| bash" to your command. The URL should change, based on the version which you are installing, so don't worry in case you spot a difference in this:

curl
https://raw.githubusercontent.com/creationix/nvm/v0.13.1/install.sh | bash

With the above command, the nvm script for the user account will be installed. The .bash_profile should be sourced so that you can begin to use this. This can be done as follows:

source ~/.bash_profile

You can then run the following command so as to ask the nvm of the Node versions which it is aware of:

nvm list-remote

A sample output from the above command is given below:

. . .
v0.10.29
v0.10.30
 v0.11.0
 v0.11.1
 v0.11.2
 v0.11.3
 v0.11.4
 v0.11.5
 v0.11.6
 v0.11.7
 v0.11.8
 v0.11.9
v0.11.10
v0.11.11
v0.11.12
v0.11.1

The choice is yours on the version of Node which you want to install. If you need to install version number v0.11.12, you just have to type the command given below:

nvm install v0.11.12

If you need to change to a different version of the nvm, you can use the following command:

nvm use version_number

You should substitute the version number in the above command. If you need to set a particular version to be the default one, just run the following command:

nvm alias default v0.101.12

If you need to verify whether the installation process ran successfully, you just have to do what we have been doing by running the command to check for the available version in your system. This is shown below:

node –version

As you have seen, there are a number of ways that you can use Node.js to run your CentOS server machine!

Conclusion

We have come to the end of this guide. CentOS 7.3 server can be used for performing a number of tasks. For instance, you can use it to install the LEMP stack which features Nginx and PHP. These are good tools for you if you want to develop web applications using your CentOS 7.3 server. It is also possible for you to install MariaDB, which works with MySQL in your CentOS server.

This will provide you with an environment for storing your data and information. You can also install Memcached in your CentOS server, and this will help you to speed up your web applications. MongoDB, which is a NoSQL database, can also be installed in CentOS, as discussed in this book. It can also provide you with a way of storing your data if you don't like the MySQL database.

If you need to do some server-side scripting on your CentOS sever, you can install Node.js, which will help you accomplish this.

www.ingramcontent.com/pod-product-compliance
Lightning Source LLC
Chambersburg PA
CBHW070902070326
40690CB00009B/1963